DiscipleWay

7 Disciplines for Maturing in Christ

Giving

Project Directors: Philip Attebery, D.Min., Steve Crawley
Writers: Scott Attebery, Paul Bullock, Ron Chesser, Clif Johnson, Joey Slayton
Content Managers: Philip Attebery, D.Min., Chris George, Ronnie Johnson, Ph.D., Jake Vandenberg
Editor: Jerome Cooper
Design Team: Ken Adams, Julie Parker, Larry Thompson

DiscipleWay Giving
ISBN 978-0-89114-477-3

DiscipleWay Giving

Contents

T U R K [E Y]

Drin R.
essio
chi
azzo
ri

Ochrida
Monastir
Kastoria

H. Varda
Seres
Kavala
Salonica
Karyes
G. of Salonika
Mt. Athos
170 m.

Thasos
Samothraki
Imbros
Dardanelles
Gallipoli
Lamsaki
Tenedos
Adramyti G.
Adra
Be

Platamona
Trikala
Yenishehr
Larissa
Volo
Pharsala
Zeitun
M. Othrys
Arta
Missolonghi
Skopelos
I.s
Skyros
264 m.

Lemnos
I.S. to C. 345 m.
C. Baba
Mytilene
G. of Smirna
Khios

Livadia
Euboea

G. of Corinth
ATHENS
Piraeus
G. of Patras
Patras
Corinth
Pyrgos
Naulia
Aegina
Poros
Hydra
Spezzia
Hermione
Polis
Tinos
Syra
Andros
Nikaria
Kalo
Naxos
Amorgo
A

G R E E C E

G. of Arkadhia
Tripolitza
Kalamata
Navarino
Modon
Sapienza
Maina
Kalavria
Monemvasia
Milo
Santorin
C. Malea
S. Nikolo
Cerigo

ante

G. of Ceroni
C. Matapan
G. of Kotolaythia
Is Cerigotto
Kisamos
Kanea
C. Krio
Sphakia
C. Spada
Suda B.
Retimo
Candia
C r e t e
Matala
Girapetra

Marseilles to Constantinople

S e a

Malta
Malta to Syra 610 m.

Marseilles to Mauritius
822 m.
Naples to P

4.0 Giving

I have shewed you all things, how that so labouring ye ought to support the weak, and to remember the words of the Lord Jesus, how he said, It is more blessed to give than to receive.
ACTS 20:35

A biblical understanding of giving begins with a proper perspective of God and our relationship to Him and the material world. Since God created everything that exists, He retains ownership of all that He gives to us. As a result, believers must learn to respect that ownership and to bear the responsibility of properly using what God has given to us. As stewards (managers of another's property) we are accountable to the Master for how we use the possessions He has placed under our responsibility. The Bible clearly identifies principles for the use of the material blessings we enjoy. First, we are to honor God by returning a portion of those blessings to Him. Then we are to use those blessings to meet our own needs. Finally, we are to put those possessions to work helping others who may not be as fortunate as we are. We must never become a slave to our possessions, but always remember that God has blessed us in order for us to be a blessing to His kingdom and to others we encounter in this life. Our true treasure is not in any earthly bank, but in heaven.

- The disciple will grow to understand the biblical basis for giving.

- The disciple will grow in the desire to give joyfully and abundantly.

- The disciple will become a steward of God's resources and help others learn to give biblically.

God's Ownership

Destination

The Bible begins with God's account of the creation of our universe. The New Testament confirms that all of this universe was made by God, and that He sustains everything. For example, if you craft a machine out of raw materials, most people will acknowledge that the machine belongs to you. No one else could rightfully claim ownership of that machine. Similarly, that is the point of recognizing God as the Creator of everything. He created all things, thus He owns all things. Thankfully He has chosen to share the goodness of His creation with us, but to maintain a proper appreciation of our possessions, we must ultimately recognize that everything we own belongs to God.

Lesson Aim: This lesson aims to lead disciples in discovering that God owns everything.

DiscipleWords

Passage: Psalm 24:1-2
Key Verse: Psalm 24:1

Preparation for the trip checklist:
- ⭕ I have prayed faithfully for myself and m~ disciple(s) and/or disciple maker.
- ⭕ I have read the lesson aim and text.
- ⭕ I have read and studied the Bible passage
- ⭕ I have memorized the key verse.

Pray together that God will open your eyes to see the greatness of His ownership of all things. Ask God to guide you as you begin this series of lessons on giving.

Walk through Psalm 24:1 together utilizing the inductive method you have learned to discover the biblical insight.

Observation

1. Who is the author?

2. Who is involved?

3. When was the book written?

4. When does this take place?

5. Are there key words or phrases (nouns, verbs)?

6. Are there words or phrases repeated?

7. Are there comparisons (like, as) or contrasts (but)?

8. Is there a cause/effect relationship (therefore, for)?

9. What form is used (parable, narrative, poetry)?

Interpretation

1. How is the passage affected by its biblical/historical context?

2. How is the passage affected by its immediate context?

3. How does this passage compare to other related passages?

4. What terms or ideas need to be researched?

5. Summarize the passage/paragraph in one sentence (main idea).

Application

1. Is there a promise to claim or truth to believe?

2. Is there an example to follow?

3. Is there an attitude to change or a sin to confess?

4. Is there a command to obey?

5. Is there a truth to believe?

6. Is there an error to avoid?

7. Is there something to praise God for?

1. Field Trip. Take a walk outside and discuss how everything belongs to God (trees, plants, animals, etc.). Be sure to ponder how even human inventions (buildings, automobiles, computers, etc.) depend on God's creation (wood, metals, elements, etc.).

2. Brainstorm. Make a list of your observations with detailed notes. Next, pray together over your lists taking turns praising God for specific details of His ownership of all creation. (For example: "Thank you, God, for creating trees that renew themselves through bearing seeds and provide wood for carpenters to use the skills you have given them to make furniture.")

3. Discussion. Spend time discussing the significance of God's ownership (why it matters) of the following items.

- Your house/apartment
- Your vehicle/transportation
- Your clothing

4. Discussion. Discuss with the other disciples the difference God's ownership makes in your possession of each item.

5. Scripture Memorization. Memorize Psalm 24:1 together.

6. Carry-Through Activity. The goal of this discipline is to impress disciples with the biblical responsibility to give and to meet the needs of others using the blessings that God has placed into their possession. To accomplish that goal, each session will advance your discipleship team through the process of selecting a need, setting back resources to meet the need, and ultimately ministering to that need with your gifts. In this session your leader will present the plan for this process.

7. Prepare to Give

- Pray to recognize God's ownership of all your possessions.
- Evaluate your current giving habits.

Evaluation

Answer the following questions.

According to Haggai 2:8, what does God own?

What does Deuteronomy 8:18 say that God does for us?

In 1 Corinthians 6:19-20 what does Paul point

out about your life?

What does the ownership of God have to do with being a giving person?

Read 1 Corinthians 13 and meditate on the topic of *love* as the basis for giving.

Get ready for the next session

Review the first lesson in the giving discipline.

Read and study Luke 18:18-30 using the inductive Bible study method.

Pray about your specific giving task as a discipleship team.

4.2

Lordship

Destination

If we accept that everything we own truly belongs to God, then we must submit all we possess to God's mastery. You may borrow a tool from your neighbor, but even while the tool is in your possession, you must respect your neighbor's ownership. You are responsible for proper maintenance, and you can't decide to dispose of the tool or sell it. When we accept Christ as our Savior, we also present everything in our lives to Him for His control. He becomes our Lord. His lordship includes mastery over our possessions and our money. If Christ is truly Lord of our lives, He must be Lord of everything.

Lesson Aim: To submit yourself and your resources to Christ's lordship.

Disciple**Words**
Passage: Luke 18:18-30
Key Verse: Luke 6:46

Preparation for the trip checklist:
- ❍ I have prayed faithfully for myself and my disciple(s) and/or disciple maker.
- ❍ I have read the lesson aim and text.
- ❍ I have read and studied the Bible passage.
- ❍ I have memorized the key verse.
- ❍ I have reviewed the previous lessons.

Recite Psalm 24:1 together from memory (from lesson 4.1).

Name the two most important things you learned from lesson 4.1 regarding ownership.

Name three authority figures in your life.

Describe how your life and resources are affected by those authority figures.

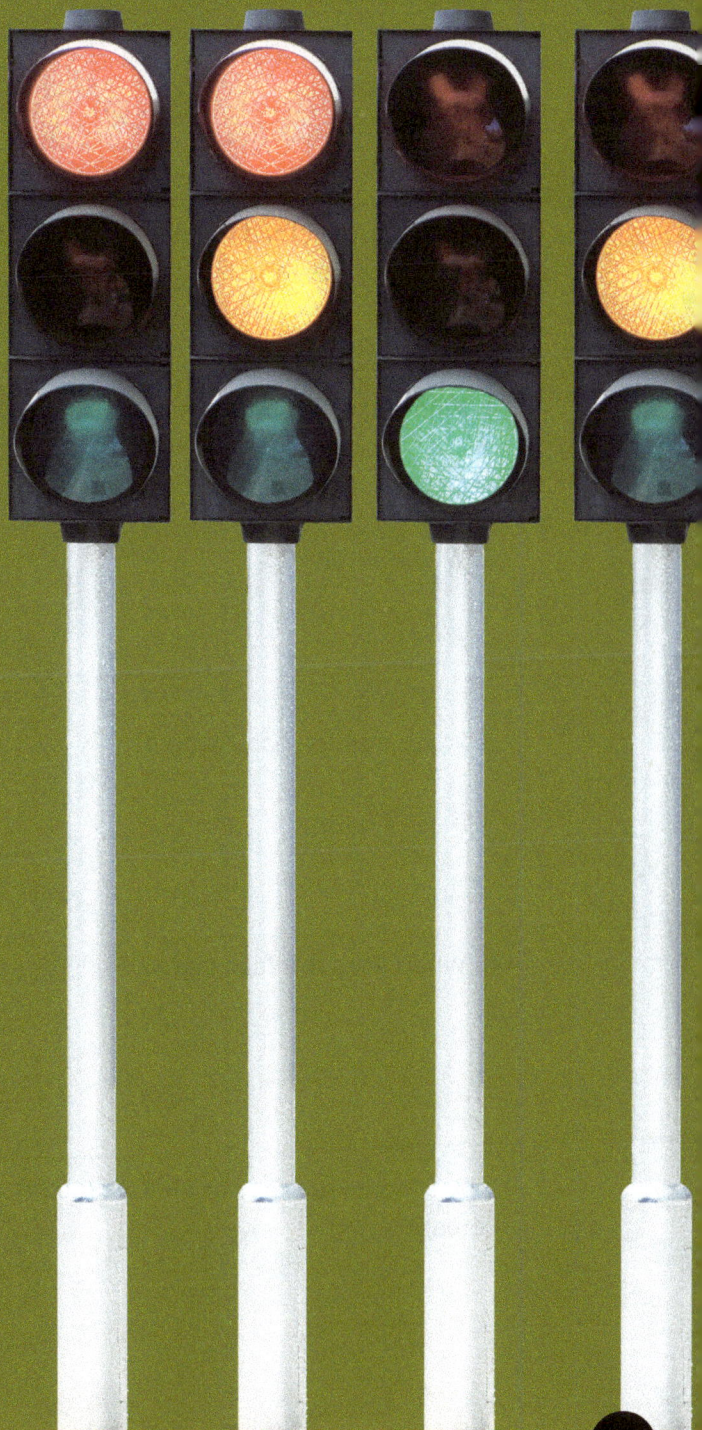

Walk through Luke 18:18-30 together utilizing the inductive method you have learned for discovering biblical truth.

Observation

1. Who is the author?

2. Who is involved?

3. When was the book written?

4. When does this take place?

4. Are there key words or phrases (nouns, verbs)?

5. Are there words or phrases repeated?

6. Are there comparisons (like, as) or contrasts (but)?

7. Is there a cause/effect relationship (therefore, for)?

8. What form is used (parable, narrative, poetry)?

Interpretation

1. How is the passage affected by its biblical/historical context?

2. How is the passage affected by its immediate context?

3. How does this passage compare to other related passages?

4. What terms or ideas need to be researched?

5. Summarize the passage/paragraph in one sentence (main idea).

Application

1. Is there a promise to claim or truth to believe?

2. Is there an example to follow?

3. Is there an attitude to change or a sin to confess?

4. Is there a command to obey?

5. Is there a truth to believe?

6. Is there an error to avoid?

7. Is there something to praise God for?

1. Brainstorm. Make a list of the five most important items you own.

How have you allowed God to take control of each of those items?

What are some ways God might want to use those possessions for His kingdom? How would you react to His requests? In light of Matthew 25:31-46, does He need to ask?

Do you feel that you could give one or more of them up if you felt God leading you to do so for the cause of His kingdom work?

Spend time praying together over each of the items on your lists. Consider committing each item to God for His purposes.

2. Carry-Through Activity. The goal of this discipline is to impress disciples with the biblical responsibility to give and to meet the needs of others using the blessings that God has placed into their possession. Use the weeks during this study to pray together about a specific need that you could meet. Seek the Lord's direction and will to reveal that need. Then in faith ask God to provide the material blessings so that you, the leader and students, can give to meet that need. Pray about this need and for God's provision each time you meet during these lessons. Then at the end of the series put your offerings together to meet the need that you have identified.

During this session spend time praying for God's wisdom and direction to identify the project your team will use as the focus of your ministry offering.

3. Prepare to Give

- Pray to recognize God's ownership of all my possessions.
- Evaluate my current giving habits.
- Recognize Christ as the master of my possessions.

Evaluation

Why do you think Jesus demands lordship?

Do you think it is a coincidence that Jesus used the young man's money and possessions to prove a point about lordship?

How does our management of money and possessions reveal the status of our relationship with Christ?

Read 1 Corinthians 13 and meditate on the topic of *love* as the basis for giving. How does our love for Christ relate to recognizing His lordship over our possessions?

Get ready for the next session

Review lessons 4-1 and 4-2.

Read and study Matthew 25:14-30 using the inductive Bible study method.

Pray about how your discipleship team will complete the specific giving task.

4.3

Stewardship

When we practice biblical stewardship, we recognize that God has given to us everything we "own" for His purpose rather than for ours. Only when we are committed to using His resources for His purposes will we find the joy He offers! In other words, stewardship recognizes God's ownership and submits to Christ's lordship, producing great joy.

Lesson Aim: Practice biblical stewardship in view of God's ownership (4.1) and Christ's lordship (4.2).

Disciple**Words**
Passage: Matthew 25:14-30
Key Verse: Matthew 25:23

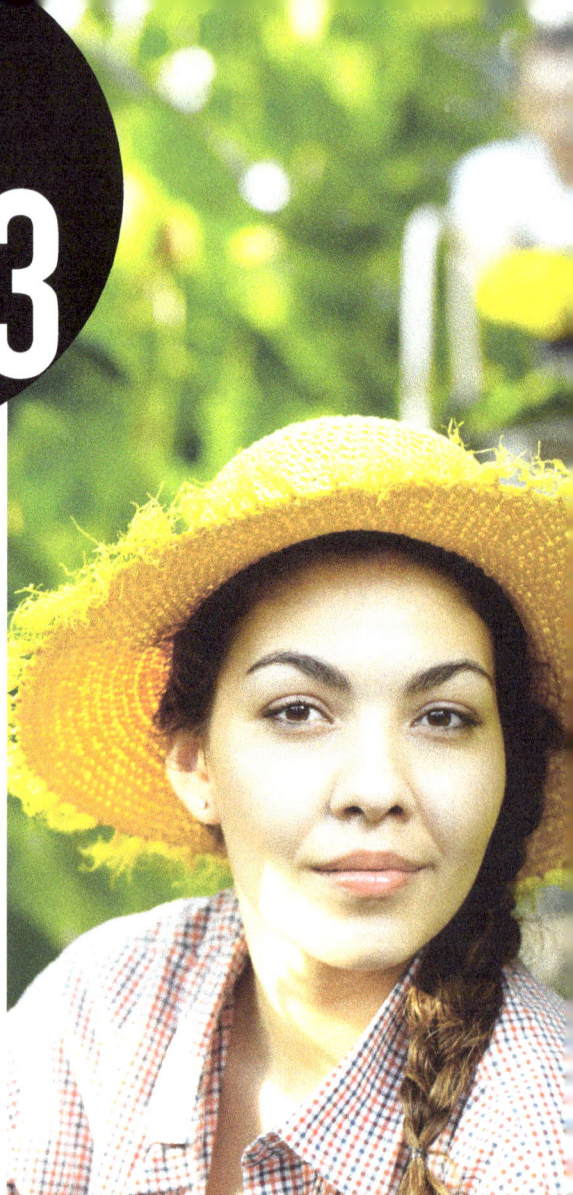

Preparation for the trip checklist:
◯ I have prayed faithfully for myself and n disciple(s) and/or disciple maker.
◯ I have read the lesson aim and text.
◯ I have read and studied the Bible passage
◯ I have memorized the key verse.
◯ I have reviewed the previous lessons.

Review last week's lesson concerning the lordship of Christ.

Using a dictionary, define *stewardship.*

Using this definition of stewardship, how would you define *biblical stewardship?*

Discuss why biblical stewardship is important to God.

Read Matthew 25:14-30 and walk through the passage together utilizing the inductive method you have learned for Bible study.

Observation

1. Who is the author?

2. Who is involved?

3. When was the book written?

4. When does this take place?

5. Are there key words or phrases (nouns, verbs)?

6. Are there words or phrases repeated?

7. Are there comparisons (like, as) or contrasts (but)?

8. Is there a cause/effect relationship (therefore, for)?

9. What form is used (parable, narrative, poetry)?

Interpretation

1. How is the passage affected by its biblical/historical context?

2. How is the passage affected by its immediate context?

3. How does this passage compare to other related passages?

4. What terms or ideas need to be researched?

5. Summarize the passage/paragraph in one sentence (main idea).

Application

1. Is there a promise to claim or truth to believe?

2. Is there an example to follow?

3. Is there an attitude to change or a sin to confess?

4. Is there a command to obey?

5. Is there a truth to believe?

6. Is there an error to avoid?

7. Is there something to praise God for?

1. Brainstorm. Share ideas with your discipleship team about how you could invest a small amount of money in a project, then give the profit, or increase, from the project to your ministry goal.

2. Carry-Through Activity. The goal of this discipline is to impress disciples with the biblical responsibility to give and to meet the needs of others using the blessings that God has placed into their possession. Use the weeks during this study to pray together about a specific need that you could meet. Seek the Lord's direction and will to reveal that need. Then, in faith, ask God to provide the material blessings so that you, the leader and students, can give to meet that need. Pray about this need and for God's provision each time you meet during these lessons. Then at the end of the series put your offerings together to meet the need that you have identified.

3. Prepare to Give

- I recognize God's ownership of all my possessions.

- I have evaluated my current giving habits.

- I recognize Christ as the master of my possessions.

- I commit to the biblical responsibility of using Christ's material blessings in a way that honors Him.

Evaluation

Why is biblical stewardship God-honoring?

Does biblical stewardship require faith? Why?

Does our stewardship place any requirement on God to multiply our material goods?

How is biblical stewardship different from smart money management?

Read 1 Corinthians 13 and meditate on the topic of *love* as the basis for giving. How does our love for Christ motivate us to be good stewards?

Get ready for the next session

Review the previous lessons in the giving discipline.

Read and study 2 Corinthians 8:1-5 using the inductive Bible study method.

Proverbs 3:9-10: Is there a commandment to keep? Is there a promise to look forward to?

How does Proverbs 11:24 reiterate the promise made in Malachi 3:10?

Matthew 6:19-21: What are the instructions in these verses? Why are these instructions given? What would this look like in your life?

What do the following verses teach us about our attitudes when it comes to giving: Matthew 23:23; 1 Corinthians 13:3; 2 Corinthians 9:7?

Pray about how your discipleship team will complete the specific giving task. Begin to make a list of needs that your discipleship team could meet.

Begin to set aside the resources that God is providing for your personal offering to your discipleship project.

Generosity

God makes it clear that we have an obligation to use our possessions to honor Him and to do good for others. It is not enough simply to say that we have given tithes and offerings and thus fulfilled our financial responsibility to God. God has blessed us so that we might be a blessing to others. When God brings needy people into our lives and He has provided us with the means to help them, we have a responsibility to be generous. Christ set that example by His own life, and we are to imitate His example in our lives.

Lesson Aim: Recognize the needs of others and give generously as God has given to you.

Preparation for the trip checklist:
❍ I have prayed faithfully for myself and my disciple(s) and/or disciple maker.
❍ I have read the lesson aim and text.
❍ I have read and studied the Bible passage.
❍ I have memorized the key verse.
❍ I have reviewed the previous lessons.

Disciple**Words**
Passage: 2 Corinthians 8:1-5, 8-15
Key Verse: 2 Corinthians 8:2

Review and summarize the previous lessons leading up to this one.

What has God so generously given to you?

Why does God give to us so generously?

How is that an example to us?

Read 2 Corinthians 8:1-5, 8-15 and answer the following questions and use the inductive method of Bible study you have learned to discover the biblical truth for this lesson.

Observation

1. Who is the author?

2. Who is involved?

3. When was the book written?

4. Are there key words or phrases (nouns, verbs)?

5. Are there words or phrases repeated?

6. Are there comparisons (like, as) or contrasts (but)?

7. Is there a cause/effect relationship (therefore, for)?

8. What form is used (parable, narrative, poetry)?

Interpretation

1. How is the passage affected by its biblical/historical context?

2. How is the passage affected by its immediate context?

3. How does this passage compare to other related passages?

4. What terms or ideas need to be researched?

5. Summarize the passage/paragraph in one sentence (main idea).

Application

1. Is there a promise to claim or truth to believe?

2. Is there an example to follow?

3. Is there an attitude to change or a sin to confess?

4. Is there a command to obey?

5. Is there a truth to believe?

6. Is there an error to avoid?

7. Is there something to praise God for?

1. Brainstorm. List examples of people or churches you have known about that were generous to give their resources to meet the needs of others.

2. Discussion. Spend some time contemplating and discussing the sincerity of your own actions in comparison to other acts of generosity you have identified.

3. Identify. Do you know of friends/families that may have a specific need? (Elderly person needing yard work, single mother needing baby sitting, etc.)? List some things that you might have that could really help with their need.

4. Research. Research ministries that you can bless with finances, time, and/or prayer. Spend time making sure you choose a ministry that will be most effective with your resources.

5. Discussion. Discuss the following quote: "Where your treasure is, there will your heart be also" (Jesus).

6. Carry-Through Activity. The goal of this discipline is to impress disciples with the biblical responsibility to give and to meet the needs of others using the blessings that God has placed into their possession. Use the weeks during this study to pray together about a specific need that you could meet. Seek the Lord's direction and will to reveal that need. Then in faith ask God to provide the material

blessings so that you, the leader and students, can give to meet that need. Pray about this need and for God's provision each time you meet during these lessons. Then at the end of the series put your offerings together to meet the need that you have identified.

During this session review the lists that your discipleship team has composed for possible projects that you can support with your offering. Make those ideas the object of prayer that God would give your team the wisdom to choose the best opportunity for you to minister.

7. Prepare to Give

- I recognize God's ownership of all my possessions.

- I have evaluated my current giving habits.

- I recognize Christ as the master of my possessions.

- I commit to the biblical responsibility of using

Christ's material blessings in a way that honors Him.

- I will give my heart to Christ and be generous with His material blessings as I seek to help others.

Evaluation

Why, as a follower of Christ, is it necessary for us to evaluate that all things are given to us by God?

Why do you think God is so generous toward you?

Should we start to see others through the eyes of God? Will that make us have a little more love and care about their needs instead of our own?

How does being generous toward others affect our walk with Christ on a daily basis?

Read 1 Corinthians 13 and meditate on the topic of *love* as the basis for giving. How does our love for Christ move us to be generous in our giving?

Get ready for the next session

Review the previous lessons in the giving discipline.

Read and study Malachi 3:6-10 and Genesis 14:17-20 using the inductive Bible study method.

Pray about how your discipleship team will choose your specific giving task. Evaluate the list of possible needs that your team has composed to determine God's direction for your project giving. Continue to set aside the money that God is providing for your personal offering to your discipleship project.

Prepare for the next lesson by writing out a simple budget that includes your total income, your current debt, and your general monthly obligations (housing, utilities, food, etc.).

4.5

Tithing

Destination

God does offer a biblical pattern for our giving. Abraham gave a tithe of his possessions to God through the priest Melchisedek. Christ is our Melchisedek, our living high priest, and we are commanded to honor Him with our offerings. Paul wrote to the believers in Corinth instructing them to give according to the measure that God had prospered them, indicating consistent, proportional giving. A tithe, ten percent, is a biblical pattern for believers to follow as they fulfill their responsibility to return to God a portion of those blessings He has given to them.

Lesson Aim: Develop a plan to give consistently in order to be continually practicing God-honoring stewardship. Give an offering through your local church next Sunday.

DiscipleWords
Passage: Malachi 3:6-10; Genesis 14:17-20
Key Verse: Malachi 3:10

Preparation for the trip checklist:
- ◯ I have prayed faithfully for myself and m disciple(s) and/or disciple maker.
- ◯ I have read the lesson aim and text.
- ◯ I have read and studied the Bible passage.
- ◯ I have memorized the key verse.
- ◯ I have reviewed the previous lessons.
- ◯ I have prepared a personal, simple budge

Using a Bible dictionary, look up the word *tithe*. According to your research, what is a tithe?

Look at Luke 11:42. In the last sentence of the verse, what does Jesus say about the Pharisees' tithing?

What was the tithe used for?

What do you think God intends for the tithe to be used for today?

31

Study Malachi 3:6-10 together.

Observation

1. Who is the author?

2. Who is involved?

3. When was the book written?

4. When does this take place?

5. Are there key words or phrases (nouns, verbs)?

6. Are there words or phrases repeated?

7. Are there comparisons (like, as) or contrasts (but)?

8. Is there a cause/effect relationship (therefore, for)?

9. What form is used (parable, narrative, poetry)?

Interpretation

1. How is the passage affected by its biblical/historical context?

2. How is the passage affected by its immediate context?

3. How does this passage compare to other related passages?

4. What terms or ideas need to be researched?

5. Summarize the passage/paragraph in one sentence (main idea).

Application

1. Is there a promise to claim or truth to believe?

2. Is there an example to follow?

3. Is there an attitude to change or a sin to confess?

4. Is there a command to obey?

5. Is there a truth to believe?

6. Is there an error to avoid?

7. Is there something to praise God for?

Walk through Genesis 14:17-20 together.

Observation

1. Who is the author?

2. Who is involved?

3. When was the book written?

4. When does this take place?

5. Are there key words or phrases (nouns, verbs)?

6. Are there words or phrases repeated?

7. Are there comparisons (like, as) or contrasts (but)?

8. Is there a cause/effect relationship (therefore, for)?

9. What form is used (parable, narrative, poetry)?

Interpretation

1. How is the passage affected by its biblical/historical context?

2. How is the passage affected by its immediate context?

3. How does this passage compare to other related passages?

4. What terms or ideas need to be researched?

5. Summarize the passage/paragraph in one sentence (main idea).

Application

1. Is there a promise to claim or truth to believe?

2. Is there an example to follow?

3. Is there an attitude to change or a sin to confess?

4. Is there a command to obey?

5. Is there a truth to believe?

6. Is there an error to avoid?

7. Is there something to praise God for?

1. Plan. If you are not tithing, make a plan to begin tithing (ten percent) as soon as possible, and to do so consistently. Make a plan to teach your children the joy of giving consistently. If you are consistently giving ten percent, make a plan to move beyond ten percent in your consistent giving, remembering the promises of Malachi 3:10.

2. Budget. Complete your simple budget planning that includes your total income, your current debt, and your general monthly obligations (housing, utilities, food, etc.), and your biblical giving. Use the chart in this session for your planning.

3. Discussion. Read and discuss the following quote from Acts 20:35: "It is more blessed to give than to receive" (Jesus). Memorize Acts 20:35 and use it as a guide for worship the next time you give your tithes and offerings.

4. Carry-Through Activity. The goal of this discipline is to impress disciples with the biblical responsibility to give and to meet the needs of others using the blessings that God has placed into their possession. Use the weeks during this study to pray together about a specific need that you could meet. Seek the Lord's direction and will to reveal that need. Then in faith ask God to provide the material blessings so that you, the leader and students, can give to meet that need. Pray about this

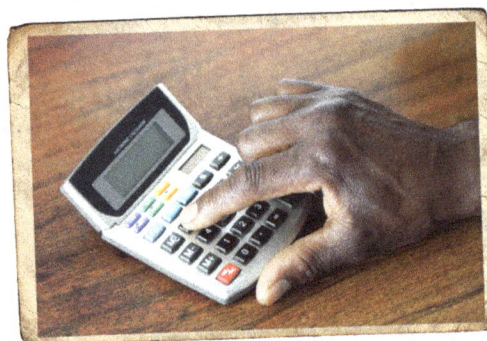

need and for God's provision each time you meet during these lessons. Then at the end of the series put your offerings together to meet the need that you have identified.

During this session select the ministry project that your discipleship team will complete with your combined offerings.

5. Prepare to Give

- I recognize God's ownership of all my possessions.
- I have evaluated my current giving habits.
- I recognize Christ as the master of my possessions.
- I commit to the biblical responsibility of using Christ's material blessings in a way that honors Him.
- I will give my heart to Christ and be generous with His material blessings as I seek to help others.

- I commit to giving ten percent of my income to the Lord, and I will begin to teach my children the joy of giving to the Lord.

Evaluation

What does inconsistent giving indicate about your heart and relationship with God?

How is your church better benefited by consistent givers?

Read 1 Corinthians 13 and meditate on the topic of *love* as the basis for giving. How does our love for Christ relate to our biblical responsibility to tithe?

Get ready for the next session

Review the previous lessons in the giving discipline.

Read and study Matthew 13:44; 6:19-21 using the inductive Bible study method.

Pray about how your discipleship team will complete the specific giving task. Begin to formulate a list of suggestions that you will discuss with your discipleship team about how you will carry out the ministry project your team has selected in lesson 4.5. Continue to set aside the money that God is providing for your personal offering to your discipleship project.

Investing

4.6

Jesus gives sound investment advice. He urges His followers to lay up their treasure in heaven so that it will be preserved. You have no doubt been urged many times to establish a sound investment plan for your future financial needs. Many people follow that advice by contributing to some kind of retirement or pension fund. But we all know how frail and undependable any savings plan is in this world. We can quickly lose everything we had counted on for the future. God does not forbid us from making wise preparation for our future in this world, in fact He commends such action. But He also teaches us that our eternal investments are far more important than the investments of this life. Our true treasure is laid up in heaven and will be the reward of how we have used God's gifts to further His kingdom in this world.

Lesson Aim: Understand the eternal benefits of spiritual investment and sacrifice, and respond with a willingness to give to build Christ's kingdom.

Destination

Disciple**Words**
Passage: Matthew 6:19-21; 13:44
Key Verse: Matthew 6:21

Preparation for the trip checklist:
- ❍ I have prayed faithfully for myself and m disciple(s) and/or disciple maker.
- ❍ I have read the lesson aim and text.
- ❍ I have read and studied the Bible passage
- ❍ I have memorized the key verse.
- ❍ I have reviewed the previous lessons.
- ❍ I reviewed Acts 20:35 during the most recent worship service I attended.

Recite Acts 20:35 together.

Review any assignment that has been given from the previous lesson.

Reveal the most difficult thing about considering and changing money habits.

Discuss with the other disciples what your greatest impact on the kingdom of Christ might have been.

Personal Testimony

I was a boy sitting in a Sunday afternoon youth meeting. The speaker that afternoon was a missionary who spoke on the needs of reaching the lost. My heart was truly broken, and I was moved to give. All the money I had to give was back at my home saved for something important. I looked at my older brother with tears rolling down my face and asked to borrow some money so that I could give half of what I had for the cause of Christ. To this day I remember the joy I had in giving that small offering and paying my brother back later that night when we got home. I don't know if I've ever met a believer from a foreign land, but I have no doubt that God used that small offering to make a big difference in the life of someone I'll meet in heaven one day. I'm thankful that the first moving of the Spirit on my life concerning giving was investing what little I had in the cause of Christ to touch someone else.

— Paul

Has God ever moved on your heart in a similar way? Share your own testimony.

Walk through Matthew 6:19-21; 13:44.

Observation

1. Who is the author?

2. Who is involved?

3. When was the book written?

4. When does this take place?

5. Are there key words or phrases (nouns, verbs)?

6. Are there words or phrases repeated?

7. Are there comparisons (like, as) or contrasts (but)?

8. Is there a cause/effect relationship (therefore, for)?

9. What form is used (parable, narrative, poetry)?

Interpretation

1. How is the passage affected by its biblical/ historical context?

2. How is the passage affected by its immediate context?

3. How does this passage compare to other related passages?

4. What terms or ideas need to be researched?

5. Summarize the passage/paragraph in one sentence (main idea).

Application

1. Is there a promise to claim or truth to believe?

2. Is there an example to follow?

3. Is there an attitude to change or a sin to confess?

4. Is there a command to obey?

5. Is there a truth to believe?

6. Is there an error to avoid?

7. Is there something to praise God for?

1. Carry-Through Activity. The goal of this discipline is to impress disciples with the biblical responsibility to give and to meet the needs of others using the blessings that God has placed into their possession. Use the weeks during this study to pray together about a specific need that you could meet. Seek the Lord's direction and will to reveal that need. Then in faith ask God to provide the material blessings so that you, the leader and students, can give to meet that need. Pray about this need and for God's provision each time you meet during these lessons. Then at the end of the series put your offerings together to meet the need that you have identified.

During this session work out the details with your discipleship team of how you will present your offering and meet the need you have chosen.

2. Prepare to Give

- I recognize God's ownership of all my possessions.

- I have evaluated my current giving habits.

- I recognize Christ as the master of my possessions.

- I commit to the biblical responsibility of using Christ's material blessings in a way that honors Him.

- I will give my heart to Christ and be generous

DONATION BOX

with His material blessings as I seek to help others.

- I commit to giving ten percent of my income to the Lord, and I will begin to teach my children the joy of giving to the Lord.

- I will identify ways to invest my gifts in the kingdom of Christ.

Evaluation

What promise does God give us concerning our sacrificial giving (Matthew 19:29)?

Read 1 Corinthians 13 and meditate on the topic of *love* as the basis for giving. How does our love for Christ motivate us to invest in His kingdom work?

Get ready for the next session

Review the previous lessons in the giving discipline.

Read and study Mark 10:29-30 using the inductive Bible study method.

Pray about how your discipleship team will complete the specific giving task. Continue to set aside the money that God is providing for your personal offering to your discipleship project. Prepare to give your offering at the next session.

Growing in Giving

4.7

In order to mature or grow in the practice of giving, we must consider what it means to lose through biblical eyes. We must be willing to understand loss as gain! That is the view Paul took as he wrote to the Philippian believers. He was willing to give up everything in this life in order for any gain that he could achieve for Christ. Nothing we can ever accumulate in this life will ever be as precious as gaining our reward in Christ. The Lord calls upon His servants to commit everything they have so that He can use their gifts to bring others to know Him. The more we grow in the grace of giving, the more we will become like Christ.

Lesson Aim: Grow in the discipline of giving even to the point of rejoicing in loss.

Disciple**Words**
Passage: Mark 10:29-30
Key Verse: Philippians 3:7

Preparation for the trip checklist:
- ❍ I have prayed faithfully for myself and my disciple(s) and/or disciple maker.
- ❍ I have read the lesson aim and text.
- ❍ I have read and studied the Bible passage.
- ❍ I have memorized the key verse.
- ❍ I have reviewed the previous lessons.
- ❍ I reviewed Acts 20:35 during the most re[cent] worship service I attended.

A loss is not always a loss. In fact, any loss for Christ's sake is no loss at all. That's why Mark 10:30 promises that any loss for Christ's sake will be repaid both in this life and in the life to come.

But the promise is for more than this life. We cannot anticipate the wonders of how God will bless us in the life to come! In order to grow in giving, we must look at loss through biblical eyes. We must be willing to understand loss as gain!

Walk through Mark 10:29-30.

Observation

1. Who is the author?

2. Who is involved?

3. When was the book written?

4. When does this take place?

5. Are there key words or phrases (nouns, verbs)?

6. Are there words or phrases repeated?

7. Are there comparisons (like, as) or contrasts (but)?

8. Is there a cause/effect relationship (therefore, for)?

9. What form is used (parable, narrative, poetry)?

Interpretation

1. How is the passage affected by its biblical/ historical context?

2. How is the passage affected by its immediate context?

3. How does this passage compare to other related passages?

4. What terms or ideas need to be researched?

5. Summarize the passage/paragraph in one sentence (main idea).

Application

1. Is there a promise to claim or truth to believe?

2. Is there an example to follow?

3. Is there an attitude to change or a sin to confess?

4. Is there a command to obey?

5. Is there a truth to believe?

6. Is there an error to avoid?

7. Is there something to praise God for?

1. List. Make a list of everything you own. As a mental exercise, imagine losing each item. How can you react with joy?

2. Act. Find items you will voluntarily lose for the gospel. Give them away as a blessing to others. Ideas may include: giving away tickets to sporting events to a family who wouldn't otherwise attend; giving away an extra vehicle to a college student in need; or giving a shopping gift card to a family in need.

3. Plan. Make a three-year plan to increase your giving. Include plans for adding an offering above your tithe and increasing it periodically.

4. Carry-Through Activity. The goal of this discipline is to impress disciples with the biblical responsibility to give and to meet the needs of others using the blessings that God has placed into their possession. Use the weeks during this study to pray together about a specific need that you could meet. Seek the Lord's direction and will to reveal that need. Then in faith ask God to provide the material blessings so that you, the leader and students, can give to meet that need. Pray about this need and for God's provision each time you meet during these lessons. Then at the end of the series put your offerings together to meet the need that you have identified.

During this session give the offering you have prepared and carry out the plan your discipleship team has created to meet the need you have chosen.

5. Prepare to Give

- I recognize God's ownership of all my possessions.
- I have evaluated my current giving habits.
- I recognize Christ as the master of my possessions.
- I commit to the biblical responsibility of using Christ's material blessings in a way that honors Him.
- I will give my heart to Christ and be generous with His material blessings as I seek to help others.
- I commit to giving ten percent of my income to the Lord, and I will begin to teach my children the joy of giving to the Lord.
- I will identify ways to invest my gifts in the kingdom of Christ.
- I will inventory my personal possessions and vow to "lose" some of them for the cause of Christ.

Evaluation

Read Hebrews 10:34. How is mature growth seen in the lives of these saints?

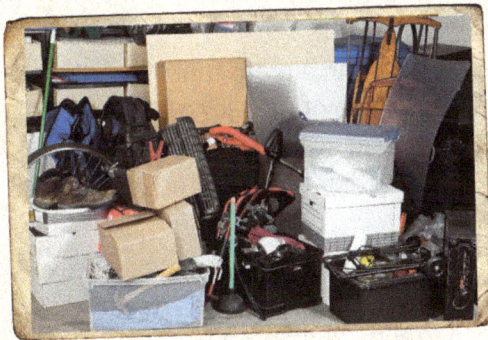

Read 1 Corinthians 13 and meditate on the topic of *love* as the basis for giving. How will our giving be affected by our growing love for Christ?

Get ready for the next session

Preview the material for the next discipline on evangelism.

Begin to identify people in your life who have not professed Christ as Savior.

Pray for those you have identified and ask God to begin to prepare their hearts to hear a gospel presentation.

Key verse for the discipline

"I have shewed you all things, how that so labouring ye ought to support the weak, and to remember the words of the Lord Jesus, how he said, It is more blessed to give than to receive" (Acts 20:35).

4.1 Key Verse

"The earth is the LORD'S, and the fulness thereof; the world, and they that dwell therein" (Psalm 24:1).

4.2 Key Verse

"And why call ye me, Lord, Lord, and do not the things which I say?" (Luke 6:46).

4.3 Key Verse

"His lord said unto him, Well done, good and faithful servant; thou hast been faithful over a few things, I will make thee ruler over many things: enter thou into the joy of thy lord" (Matthew 25:23).

4.4 Key Verse

"How that in a great trial of affliction the abundance of their joy and their deep poverty abounded unto the riches of their liberality" (2 Corinthians 8:2).

4.5 Key Verse

"Bring ye all the tithes into the storehouse, that there may be meat in mine house, and prove me now herewith, saith the LORD of hosts, if I will not open you the windows of heaven, and pour you out a blessing, that there shall not be room enough to receive it" (Malachi 3:10).

4.6 Key Verse

"For where your treasure is, there will your heart be also" (Matthew 6:21).

4.7 Key Verse

"But what things were gain to me, those I counted loss for Christ" (Philippians 3:7).

www.ingramcontent.com/pod-product-compliance
Lightning Source LLC
Chambersburg PA
CBHW081242020426
42331CB00013B/3263